ISBN 978-0-578-77597-5
Publisher: For His Sake Publishing Group
Houston, Texas 77044

Be Healed

'YOUR TRAUMA, IS JUST A COMMA'

Tonya Dixon

REVIEWS & ACCOLADES

Tonya Dixon will literally change the way you think and look at life. She is one of the most beautiful person's I have ever been blessed to meet. Tonya's energy is infectious. Her faith in God is unwavering. Her heart to serve and do for others is inspiring and her impact is unmeasurable. I have learned and continue to learn so much from Tonya. She has changed my life and filled my heart. You can find Tonya dancing while teaching kids, singing while feeding the homeless, speaking on the RBRW show which she is a co-host or reading her book, *"T'Was The Night Christ Was Born!"* Tonya Dixon is one of a kind. She is a radiant light that brightens up the world. She is a gift to all of us and so is her newest release, *"Be Healed".*
With love and gratitude,
- Jacquelyn Aluotto
RBRW | Where Beauty, Glamour, and Entertainment Meet Social Responsibility ™ and Break The Cycle Founder

"Be Healed" is a powerful devotional that will impact you physically, emotionally and spiritually! WOW! Tonya hits the core needs of today's Christian through Scripture-based writing, poignant prayers and thoughtful insight. In this season of so much change and challenge, this book is an amazing asset. It's easy to read but hard to put down. It's beautifully written and illustrated. I recommend it as a "must have" for the next leg of your journey!
Dr. Teresa Hairston
Founder/Publisher emeritus, Gospel Today Magazine
CEO, Books2liveby.com

Get your passport, boarding pass, carry-on and prepare to take a life changing journey. This pilgrimage will take you through a mother's worst nightmare and the turbulence of her traumatic experience. Through the lens of faith, Tonya embraces her trial and fervently looks for God's grace to comfort her. She exemplifies great faith and complete reliance on God's healing hand to guide her along the way. Every traveler's hope is to arrive at their destination safely. Be Healed is an intimate devotional that gives biblical principles and applicable steps to help elevate your spirit from brokenness, emptiness, neglect to the desired destination...healed.
- Sheretta M. West
First Lady of The Church Without Walls
An Executive Producer, Editor & Author

REVIEWS & ACCOLADES

Strength is not about how much you can handle before you break. It's about how much you can endure after you've been broken. God uses the fire in our development to mend our brokenness and to prove our tensile strength. We are so proud of you.

 - Mom and Dad

I am a firm believer that we can all "grow through" as we "go through". On the road to total healing one must first accept that you are experiencing either God's will for your life or what He has allowed. There are many common threads between the nuggets of knowledge to be gleaned during the healing process. So no matter what your curvy path of life has led you to and through, I admonish readers to meditate on the referenced scripture, internalize the poised prayers and embrace journaling as a vehicle to carry you to your healing. I have been afforded the invaluable gift of sailing through life with the consistent model of the many attributes of my mother including her strategic guidance both directly and indirectly; and mostly the calculated exposure to her divine presence. I am certain that through your devoted engagement with this journal you can experience healing in a myriad of ways to reach your destination of "ultimate healing".

 - Tyam Richard

Our wounds are often the openings into the best and most beautiful part of our lives. Embrace the journey and expect the joy of "Being Healed!"

 - Max Bozeman

I recommend this devotional journal to every female who is ready to heal from life's hurts and pain. This journal will help you discover both purpose and value after disappointments, mistakes, and failures.
Get ready to Be Healed!

 - Tim Dixon

"Be Healed" grants me permission to call by name every experience that has caused me trauma and gives me the applicable Scripture and daily exercise to equip me for war against the enemies' deception to keep me stuck in the cycle of pain.

 - Carlondria Dixon

Our brokenness may not be the same, but we all know brokenness! Tonya Dixon in her absolute transparency, in this book, has allowed God to use every ounce of her pain, affliction and brokenness to aid me in my own healing. **Let your healing begin!**

 - Chris Dixon

Dedication

I dedicate this book to those closest to me because my life's experiences became theirs. They were infected with all that affected and impacted my life.

My plight became theirs:
My parents, James and Carrol Dixon;

My siblings, Bishop James Dixon, II, DMin, Pastor Tim Dixon and my songbird sister, Carlondria Dixon aka "Sister";

To these two who live within every one of my heart beats:
My daughter, Tyam who is allowing God to heal her through her hurt, anguish, and disappointments of systematic biases;

My son, Max Bozeman, II who we believe right now is healed of colon cancer at his tender age of 36;

And yes, to my Chris Boze, whose spirit continues to be alive in me and reminding me of the faithfulness of God, not just during delightful times, but also during the toughest of times.

Acknowledgements

To my sister who I've been blessed with through the love of my brother, Christie Steverson Dixon. I am forever indebted to you for extending yourself and discovering "the more" God has put in you and your willingness to dispense it generously in this journey you've embarked upon with me by co-producing and co-publishing, *"Be Healed"* ♥ and *"T'was the Night Christ was Born"*, both authored by yours truly.

To my beloved sister, Barbra Jones, whose love and affection has helped to create my village (family extension) and whose modeling of excellence has helped to shape my ideology - no matter what, never compromising excellence by settling for mediocrity. Yes, you're a renowned educator and administrator whose expertise and unequivocal passion and style has led to your footprints being imprinted from the gulf coast to the east coast. I'm so grateful your sovereign path has led you into the birthing room of "Be Healed" with me. You're my doula in this birthing. You've provided me emotional, physical, and educational support making this birthing experience more memorable, empowering and deliverable to those seeking to *"Be Healed"*!

To know you, Virginia Smith is to love and respect you. Sis. Virginia, as I respectfully call you, brings so much value to me. While God has blessed us with many similarities, He's likewise blessed us with unique differences. I operate predominantly through the direction of the right hemisphere of the brain, while you're guided through the left hemisphere. Just as these hemispheres must operate interdependently in our brains to bring balance into our lives, so is it with you in my life and in the delivery of *"Be Healed."* You're my viewer who sees through different lenses. You're my reader who analyzes and processes more methodically than emotionally. You're a member of my chief editing team whose expertise qualifies you and whose belief in the ministry of this message has inspired you in giving yourself to it. I'm truly grateful to God for the multiplied blessing He's given me through you!

Foreword by Dr. James Dixon, II

For each of us, life is a journey taken in the blind. We discover our lives as we go. No one gets a path that is well paved and well lit. There are dark places, potholes, and collisions. Some that are caused by others, and frankly, some by our own reckless living. No matter who's at fault, the result is still pain! This is why "Be Healed" is such a timely and necessary resource.

We live around and we live with wounded people. In fact, we are at times, the wounded person others are trying to live with. It can be excruciating. Why? Well, I'm sure you've heard the phrase, "hurt people hurt people." How? Hurting people are often steered by the emotions connected to their painful experiences. Which means everything and everybody gets viewed and evaluated through the lens of a victim whose perspective is suspicion. Unhealed emotions lead to the dominance of fear, the prevalence of anger, and can lead to reticence and paranoia.

The collateral damage done to relationships due to this truth is beyond measurable. An array of ruptured relationships litter the human landscape due to unhealed people. Failed marriages. Disconnected siblings. Children estranged from parents. Family feuds that persist through generations. Can you relate to this? Unfortunately, most broken people never get healed. That's because they often don't believe they can be. Or, they've never had a guide to aide them on the healing journey. Thanks to this author, help is now in your hands.

When you begin to read this journal, you'll know at once that you've picked up rare content. You'll feel the power of Tonya's authenticity and be compelled by her transparency. But most importantly, you'll be transformed by using this tool as a healing remedy. She makes it clear that Jesus is the healing power. So will be a walk with you and the Lord. His words, His grace, His strength to forgive and be forgiven are all accessed through the instructive lessons in this book.

Without delay, get started, and go all the way. Not only will you feel better, you'll make others feel better around you. Most importantly, you'll come to know the liberating power that positions you to live out God's highest purpose for your life. Healed people are healthier and happier. Thank God, for using Tonya to pen these pages. They are medicine for the soul.

Tonya Dixon, is one of the brightest lights on the planet. In addition to being my sister, she's a minister of hope. Being healed has turned whet pain into incredible power!

The Author's Story

I am a blessed recipient of God's gracious gift of healing! Having encountered so many people filled with hurt, anguish, sickness, pain, grief and brokenness as me, it has become more apparent that trauma has not only inundated people within my sphere of reach, but also far beyond my physical scope and touch. This thick cloud of devastation, with no break of sunshine, glooms over all of us at various times of life. I have been commissioned by the Holy Spirit to offer myself as an exhibit of the healing power of Jehovah Rapha, the God who heals.

Looking at my present state in life, you would (might) be quite overtaken viewing the historical timeline of my life. The truth is, my present reality is certainly not indicative of all I've been through. All I can say is, ...but for the grace of God!

I've experienced pain, hurt, anguish, resentment and brokenness. As a teen who was raped, I'm well acquainted with the feeling of emptiness and lifelessness. Deep sorrow was my shadow after aborting my first pregnancy. Heartbreak and anguish invaded my life through the betrayal of my first love, who I began my intimate journey with as a 10th grade student. We married and birthed our family of three. I devoted my life to him over 25 years with it ending in divorce and leaving me to start from ground zero. In this process, it was revealed our home was in foreclosure and I had a matter of days to move out before being locked out. I had to walk away, not just from a house, but a home I had just completed remodeling to meet my heart's desire with an inheritance from my God-mother, Maw-maw, who always put forth every effort to ensure my life was as happy as could be. Sometimes when it rains, it does pour. My world really shook when my youngest son got caught up in the criminal judicial system simultaneously facing 3 charges resulting in up to a 33-year sentence for each offense. As though this was not enough, subsequently, I found myself having to move in with relatives, lost my vehicle and was forced to carpool to work and church. Thank God for my sister and BFF, who allowed me to borrow their vehicles to drive hundreds of miles away every weekend to go love on, support and minister to my son and all those in such a dark place in need of The Light to show up. After a decade in the judicial system, I was overjoyed to have my son come home to me – only to be murdered a year after getting off papers. Oh, I didn't share the inflictions of sicknesses and disease in my body. In my early 20's, I began my battle with breast challenges when mammograms, ultrasounds, and inconclusive biopsies baffling my physicians and surgeon began. I suffered a miscarriage that almost took me out because the pregnancy was in my fallopian tubes and pregnancy tests at the doctor's office repeatedly came back negative for weeks until I could no longer even walk. Bowed over to my knees, my grandfather rushed me to the hospital where it was determined I was 5 months pregnant.

In my early 30's, rheumatoid arthritis set up in my body. I became an invalid not able to use my hands or feet. I had to depend on assistance to eat, drink, dress, do my hair and make-up, and to bathe. I was only mobile in a wheelchair. Yes, this was me. My very active lifestyle all changed in one day. I have lost two established businesses and much more. I have just shared with you a snippet of my life less this journal becomes an autobiography. I believe you'll agree from what's been presented, that I am a viable witness whose truth has been fact checked. I am only making this known to you because I have willingly placed my life back into my Master's hand for Him to use me to help you heal!

Oh! But to know me today! You will meet a successful single woman who has embraced the flavor of her present status and is experiencing living life more abundantly!

I am considered the adhesive that keeps our family bonded. Having weathered a season of unexplainable illness and undesirable circumstances, I am known as a "Prayer Warrior." I am called to lay hands on, anoint and pray others through their toughest times. My motherly nature, heart of compassion, transparency of truth, and nonjudgmental spirit, makes me relatable, resourceful and relevant- drawing people to me for encouragement, support, and spiritual guidance as a mentor. God has used me as a great influencer and light through my surrendered service in His ministry as I've been able to direct and redirect the lives of countless children, youth, marrieds, singles (both men and women alike), and families through ministry leadership capacity - directing, training and equipping the children of God. God in His redemptive nature and love has held me up through my most adverse times and has made me especially loving and compassionate for children and families.

I am grateful God has chosen to use me to be a steward of and minister to thousands of children and families during my 32 years as a Private Christian School Director and Educator. He has elevated me to become a sought-after professional trainer, coach and mentor to my colleagues in the Early Childhood Profession. He has anointed the work of my hands generated through my ingenuity to establish programs not only appreciated for its success by parents, but well respected by the scholarly and experts. One notable recognition has come through the partnership with Walden University to feature myself and Dominion Prep's program in a documentary shared with students in their doctoral program and their nationwide broadcast campaign.

I believe my teenage trauma, as well as my parents always being present to speak in ways I wasn't able to, contributes to me serving as an advocate for children locally and nationally to Capital Hill among Legislators. My daily quest to live each day to bless others has led me to minister with no bars held with compassion and passion. I have experienced the pain of having a brother and child incarcerated which is why I continue to minister in women's and men's prisons. I have established and led the mission feeding over 3K children and families each week during the COVID-19 pandemic. I have organized free COVID-19 Testing Centers in impoverished communities. I'm referred to as, "The Go-To Person" for whatever the need because although I might not be able to directly help, I am diligent in utilizing my vast contacts to provide the resources needed to assist.

I am a children's author, a playwright, a theater arts actress, director, and producer. Additionally, I am a co-host on a nationally viewed talk show – Real Beauty Real Women (RBRW). My journey is not over. I do not have all of my I's dotted or T's crossed as one may begin to think. I am a college student in pursuit of my Bachelor of Arts degree, while concurrently enrolled in a certification program with degreed, professional educators.

With all of my accomplishments and accolades, I am most blessed and proud to be the mother of Tyam, Max and Christon and grandmother of five to Kingston, Kaiya, Mahari, Marli and Max Christon.

As my journey continues, I dare not give you the impression that the road is easy. Are there thorns in this bed of roses pricking me along the way? You bet! But, I am being true to you and true to God's calling on my life to evangelize the world. "Be Healed" will definitely be my best traveling partner!

I encourage you to make "Be Healed" your traveling companion of choice!

Be Healed

Tanya

As life enters this world, it's defined in trimester stages. It is often packaged with discomforts and challenges causing you to altar your normal routine and lifestyle. Sometimes increased agony of your present reality, prevalent emotional devastation, depression, heightened blood pressure leads to out of control stress all while carrying something that is meant to be a blessing to you and the world. After carrying full term, a different form of discomfort, agony and pain streaks through your body testing every essence of your being - your physical, mental and spiritual endurance. It seems you're dying as you're birthing. Suddenly in one breath while inhaling, your body is overwhelmed with excruciating pain, but before exhaling, you're blessed with indescribable release, relief, and a new creature!

This my friend is very similar to what we experience in our most devastated places in life. We go through carrying the problem, enduring the agony, discomfort, and what seems the most unbearable pain that's ripping the life out of us. Although we would wish to abort it, we must carry it to full term. The premonition in your spirit will let you know when you're moving from stage to stage. So, I admonish you to not use "Be Healed" as another piece of literature for a good read, or you simply go through the motion of using it as a daily routine or looking for a quick fix. Be true to yourself, meditate and allow the words, thoughts and prayers to marinate in your spirit invoking a personal experience with the greater power beyond yours to give you the will, strength, confidence and courage to allow the new you to be birthed. The world is awaiting your arrival. *Come on, it's time for you to Be Healed!*

Let's Prepare For Takeoff

Have you ever taken a flight and had either a layover or had to change planes? Perhaps yours was not a flight. It could have been a school bus or some other mode of transportation to get you from one place to another, but where you had to share it with others joining you along your route with the destination being the same place.

I'd like you to understand that embarking on your healing journey, the navigated path for you may very well not be the charted course others have taken or are on; but, don't fret. If you'll allow the Command Center to map out your course on your privately charted flight and the Pilot responsible for getting you to your destination to take control, you're sure to arrive safely.

Let me introduce the Crew Members:
God is the Chief Commander Traffic Specialist who has mapped out your charted course. He's the one most able to know and see all this flight will take you through, needed equipment and possible repairs along the journey as well as necessary rerouting to avoid calamity.

The Holy Spirit is the Pilot. He is navigating you along your journey, helping you to know, understand and adhere to His instructions in order to arrive, like myself and others, to your desired destination - your place of healing.

Unfortunately, because of unforeseen elements and unpredictable forecasts, no definitive time can be provided when you'll reach your destination. Sometimes, you may encounter a layover. If so, please remember layovers are temporary places and not your final destination. If you get distracted and remain there longer than you should, you will likely miss your next scheduled boarding.

So, in using this God-crafted vehicle, **"Be Healed"**, you're permitted to bring along all the baggage you believe is necessary. You must have proper identification that will remind you to be the truest **you** to yourself. You must give up your authority of navigating yourself and trust the Pilot who's following the directives from the command center.

Beware that some baggage may become unnecessary weight during your journey and will need to be ejected. Please sign the authorization for automatic ejection now!

_____   _____
Signature   Date

The flight attendant is going to provide some special instructions as we prepare for take off. Please take your seat, fasten your seatbelt and give her your undivided attention. Flight Attendant please prepare our passengers for take-off.

- Please be sure you have boarded the correct flight. This flight's destination is Healing. Although we will experience some unpleasant conditions, you must trust that we've been given the best path to travel to get you there safely.

- Please be sure you remain seated with your seatbelt fastened, in your space specifically designed for you to have privacy during our flight. The Pilot will announce when it is safe to move about.

- Please follow the instructions as they appear in your journal.

  1. **"Your Prayer of Faith"**: Honestly express yourself to God and allow Him to express Himself to you. He only speaks truth so, do not worry.

  2. **"Your Faith Work"**: This space is devoted to your action plan to do what God is saying. Some tasks will be more challenging than others, but you can certainly make it through.

  3. **"Your Faith Praise"**: By faith (belief in the expected outcome before it occurs) praise and thank God for your place in the journey and for each marker that shows you're getting closer to your destination, your healing.

PASSENGER RECEIPT : OF 2

Boarding Pass

First Class

1A

Departure Gate: Broken
Arrival Gate: Healed

Now we're ready for take-off...

"Heal me, O Lord, and I will be healed; save me and I will be saved, for you are the one I praise."
~ Jeremiah 17:14

Prayer of Purpose:

Dear God, my Lord, who has the right of ownership over my life, I cry out to You because I have been stricken with sin sickness. I've indulged in things that looked good, sounded good, tasted good and felt good - soothing my emotions and boosting my ego. I'm experiencing the great fall that pride causes, my sin disease is eating me alive; so, I pray that You will heal me, O Lord, and if You do so I know I will be healed. Save me, O Lord, especially from my own recklessness that leads to my demise and I shall be saved. It's You I will honor, by surrendering my life to You. It's You I will praise and declare Your great healing as the balm in Gilead that healed my sin sick soul. In the healing name of Jehovah Rapha I pray, AMEN.

Your Prayer of Faith

Date: _____

_____

_____

_____

_____

_____

_____

_____

_____

Your Faith Work

Date: _____

_____

_____

_____

_____

_____

_____

_____

Your Faith Praise

Date: _____

_____

_____

_____

_____

_____

_____

_____

"Is anyone among you sick? Let them call the elders of the church to pray over them and anoint them with oil in the name of the Lord. And the prayer offered in faith will make the sick person well; the Lord will raise them up. If they have sinned, they will be forgiven."
~ James 5:14-15

Prayer of Purpose:

Dear God who hears the prayers of Your children, You have instructed us to call upon the elders of the church, those who have the special gifting of prayer and are mature in the faith to pray over us. So, in obedience to Your instruction, I submit myself into their hands to pray over me, anointing me with oil. I understand the healing power is not merely in the oil, but in the power of the unseen active work of the Holy Spirit to heal me. I believe as the elders pray over me, touching my ailing body with anointed oils, their faith along with mine will invoke the divine intervention of Jesus to heal me. Thank You that I'm not in this alone and when I'm too weak or weary, the elders of the church will pray over me in faith and I will regain strength in my body and in my faith. In the gracious name of Jesus who made this gift available to me, AMEN.

Your Prayer of Faith   Date:_____

_____

_____

_____

_____

_____

_____

_____

Your Faith Work   Date: _____

_____

_____

_____

_____

_____

_____

Your Faith Praise   Date: _____

_____

_____

_____

_____

_____

_____

"Worship the LORD your God, and his blessing will be on your food and water. I will take away sickness from among you..."
~ Exodus 23:25

"God is great, God is good let us thank Him for our food. By His hands we must be fed; give us Lord our daily bread." As children, many grew up reciting this prayer called "Grace" over every meal consumed. Knowing who God is and how He performs on our behalf should be enough to stir up our worship to Him. God placed in the earth all we have need of for consumption to nourish our physical body. All things come of thee O Lord; so, we slow down in our rapid pace to worship You for being such a great and gracious God. Your blessings to provide daily bread for our physical man is quite relatable to us because we quickly recognize the symptoms/signs that warn us when our bodies have been deprived of it. On the other hand, deceptive tactics of the enemy lead us to believe that our spirit man needs just a little bit more of the poison he's concocted to make us feel what we are consuming is all we have need of for our satisfaction. But, when we're delivered, our appetites change. We regurgitate and reject that poison the enemy presents and acquire a hunger and thirst for righteousness and for the food and drink that are blessed. When we drink from the well that will never run dry - which is the water of life – and, when we consume the bread of life daily (God's Word), it purges and cleanses us, and sickness and disease leaves out of us. Feast on God's Word, therein lies your healing.

Prayer of Purpose:

Dear God, *You have provided for us the fountain of life so that when we drink, we'll never thirst again. You've given us provisions of daily bread to nourish our soul that hungers for righteousness. Thank You, God, our Jehovah Jireh. Thank You that the water purifies our body as it flushes out impurities, toxins and waste which cause sickness and disease to settle in our bodies. Thank You that the water also transports nutrients where they are needed for healing and making us stronger. Thank You for every seed, herb and all that are produced in the earth for consumption and nourishment which contain every source of vitamin, mineral and element so we are healthy, well and whole. We worship You God because of who You are. You are God, Yeshua, the God who created all things for our well-being and pleasure so, we worship You. You are our healer, Jehovah Rapha. You quench our thirst and fulfill our hunger because You've taken care of all our needs. We thank You, in Jesus' name, AMEN.*

Your Prayer of Faith

Date: _____

_____

_____

_____

_____

_____

_____

_____

_____

Your Faith Work

Date: _____

_____

_____

_____

_____

_____

_____

_____

Your Faith Praise

Date: _____

_____

_____

_____

_____

_____

_____

_____

"TEARS"

It's been said that, *"Your tears are only a temporary*
release of your pain, sorrow and grief."
Temporary! Only temporary! Did I hear you say?
When I'm curled up in a fetal position, balling, and
praying for all of this to be taken away.
I don't want just a temporary release; I want to be free.
It's also been said very matter of factly,
your tears are made up with the natural elements
of water, salt and oil
and have purpose unbeknownst to many.
So don't suck it up and dry your eyes so fast,
especially if you're ready to wash away the past.
No matter the underlying condition of your grief
that has your head hanging low and you feeling weak in
your knees,
Hang on!
Every teardrop has a magic healing potion mixed within
that will give you renewed strength to begin again.
So let the tears flow no matter how they sting your face
because my friend you're on the brink of a brighter day.
TEARS

Psalm 30:5 says, "joy comes in the morning."

"So do not fear, for I am with you; do not be dismayed, for I am your God. I will strengthen you and help you; I will uphold you with my righteous right hand." ~ Isaiah 41:10

When things seem to crumble around us like a domino effect, it causes our eyes to widened and our mouths to drop with fear as we see things slipping through our fingers. When things begin to deteriorate internally and your health is declining be it physically, mentally, or emotionally with the uncertainty that accompanies it - it makes your way dismal and fogged with fear, worry and doubt, but remember God has given us a promise of reassurance we can trust. He says, you're not in this thing alone for I am with you and I am your God. Do you remember the story of Jesus being out at sea with the disciples and a bad storm arose? Jesus was down in the boat asleep and the disciples were up scurrying frantically because they thought surely this would wipe them out. They did as we often do, they forgot who was on board with them. In their panicking state, they cried out to Jesus. He awoke and said, "Why are you so afraid?"

Today, He's asking you the same question and His answer remains the same: ***"There's no need to fear, I am in control. In your weakened state, I will strengthen you."*** *No matter how the storm might be raging in your life and the winds are causing the waves to beat upon you, seemingly to overtake you, be assured I am a very present help in the time of trouble. I will help you! In my right hand you are secured, protected and preserved. May this reassurance bring calm to your storm. I hear the Master saying,* ***Peace be still!***

Prayer of Purpose:

Dear God, my Father, who is omnipotent, I thank You that today I believe You're going to speak to the things causing turbulence in my life. I believe in Your ability to speak peace and there will be peace. Thank You for reassuring me through this Word to activate my faith to unleash Your power. Thank You that every weapon formed to destroy me by the evil one will not prosper. I trust You with my life. I trust You to super rule over every power that tries to grip the reign of my mind, my body and my spirit causing me to live in a terrifying state and headed to doom. Thank You that as the storms of life rage in my life, my soul is anchored in You. I'm safe and secured under the shadows of Your wings and here I can take refuge from all danger. Thank You so much Jehovah Elohim, my Protector. In Your Son, Jesus' mighty name, I pray, AMEN.

Your Prayer of Faith

Date: _____

_____

_____

_____

_____

_____

_____

_____

Your Faith Work

Date: _____

_____

_____

_____

_____

_____

_____

_____

Your Faith Praise

Date: _____

_____

_____

_____

_____

_____

_____

_____

"Do I Want a Pity Party?"

Do I want a pity party?
No, I just want to know, why me?
Sickness in my body with diagnosis
of this incurable disease
After all, my prayer has always been,
Lord let me live life happy, healthy and free.
So the answer is no, I don't want a pity party
I just want to know, why me?

I've devoted my life trying to live right in Christ
Caring for the needy, helping all I could,
forgiving and loving all as He told me I should.
And now, I find myself in this terrible plight.
I'm literally in a fight for my life.
Do I want a pity party?
No, I just want to know, why me?

Am I disgusted, confused and perplexed?
You bet!
Do I want a pity party?
No, I just want to know, why me?

"Not only so, but we also glory in our sufferings, because we know that suffering produces perseverance; perseverance, character; and character, hope. And hope does not put us to shame, because God's love has been poured out into our hearts through the Holy Spirit, who has been given to us. You see, at just the right time, when we were still powerless, Christ died for the ungodly."
~ Romans 5:3-6

"Therefore we do not lose heart. Though outwardly we are wasting away, yet inwardly we are being renewed day by day. For our light and momentary troubles are achieving for us an eternal glory that far outweighs them all. So we fix our eyes not on what is seen, but on what is unseen, since what is seen is temporary, but what is unseen is eternal."
~ 2 Corinthians 4:16-18

"But I will restore you to health and heal your wounds,' declares the LORD because you are called an outcast, Zion for whom no one cares." ~ Jeremiah 30:17

Prayer of Purpose:

Great and mighty God, I acknowledge it is only in You I may experience being reestablished, free from illness and injury in my physical state, my mental state and my spiritual state. I pray to be healed of every side effect I'm enduring. I've tried to concoct self-remedies as though I might be able to prove I'm somewhat wiser than not only the experts in medicine, but also You, the Great Physician, who's wisest of all and knows just what needs to be ordered and prescribed to cure me. Forgive me for acting as though I knew what was best or better for me by even relying on things I knew were a temporary fix or a quick remedy for my discomfort and pain.

Thank You, Jahveh (Your name that represents You as the Godhead) for reminding me that You are my Creator, the One who designed the physiology of my body. You're the One who is omniscient, there are no limits to what You know and no boundaries that can prevent You from knowing anything about everything. Therefore, You know my wounds are so much deeper than the superficial scarring visible to others. Because You know everything there is to know about every thing, You know that which makes my present state unhealthy. You are able to direct attention to the specific area of the illness and not just treat my symptoms. You are able to heal me of the disease that's causing the disorder in my body, mind, and spirit. As I am healed, You're also able to cure me of all symptoms indicative of what you've delivered me from. Thank You for doing this for me Jehovah!

Almighty God, the affects of my wounds would have certainly caused me to be an outcast and to remain in the original state of Zion, a dry place of waste and ruins because wounded people wound others, hurting people hurt others, inflicted people inflict others. But as Zion is also symbolic of the raised-up place, thank You for healing me and raising me up. Now because my health is restored, I'm strengthen and able to glorify You by being an ocular demonstration of Your restoration power. Thank You, in the restorative name of Jesus, AMEN.

Your Prayer of Faith

Date: _____

_____

_____

_____

_____

_____

_____

_____

Your Faith Work

Date: _____

_____

_____

_____

_____

_____

_____

_____

Your Faith Praise

Date: _____

_____

_____

_____

_____

_____

_____

_____

"Nevertheless, I will bring health and healing to it; I will heal my people and will let them enjoy abundant peace and security."
~ Jeremiah 33:6

In spite of it all, God says, He will bring health and healing to your "It Thing!" Can you identify your "It Thing" that inflicts an unhealthy state of being in your body, in your emotions (mind) and/or in your spirit? The truth is, all of us have at least one "It Thing." If we'll keep it 📖, we have multiple "It Things" that are causing sickness in our bodies preventing us from having a quality life; sickness in our mind infecting us with thoughts and behaviors causing self-inflicted deterioration; and sickness in our spirit resulting in us becoming broken and severed from The Source, God - who makes us a healthy, whole person. Our unhealthy state makes our bodies act out causing anxiety attacks, rage or behavioral disorders, confusion, frustration, anger, bitterness and hopelessness. Our healthy state in Christ gives us a peace that surpasses all understanding and an unspeakable joy that doesn't dissipate even during our most perplexed circumstances. We become secure in our own skin and secure in the very essence of our being. We have full assurance of faith, having our hearts sprinkled clean from an evil conscience and our bodies washed with pure water. We thank God that our "It Thing" did not prevent us from being justified by faith. We thank God because we have peace with Him - through our Lord Jesus Christ. **"Nothing can separate us from the love of God. Death cannot! Life cannot! The angels of darkness cannot! No other power in this world or of this world cannot! Hard things now or in the future cannot!"**

Prayer of Purpose:

Dear God, *I thank You for being my mind regulator. As I sit thinking of this ordeal, my "It Thing", that's really enough to make me lose my mind. I'm so thankful that You are freeing me from its captivity. Thank You for giving me the courage to confront it with confidence in Your power to heal and deliver me from it. I know no matter how much power my "It Thing" has had over me causing depression, pain, sickness, sorrow, and grief as I was searching for a way to escape what I didn't like about how I was feeling, it caused me to take on behaviors where I've inflicted more of the same on myself. Thank You for having mercy on me. Thank You for healing me. Thank You for loving me into the security of Your graces where the devil in hell and all his agents, schemes and tactics cannot pluck me out of Your safety. Thank You, Jehovah El-Elohim for being my strong protector and my peace. AMEN!*

Your Prayer of Faith   Date: _____

_____

_____

_____

_____

_____

_____

_____

_____

Your Faith Work   Date: _____

_____

_____

_____

_____

_____

_____

_____

_____

Your Faith Praise   Date: _____

_____

_____

_____

_____

_____

_____

_____

_____

"This Is Not the End"

Life is filled with swift transition
And trials do come on every hand.
You're left with unanswered questions,
perplexed about the things you
just don't understand.

The pressures of life weigh heavy upon you
Entrapping you in a lonely place.
And what you must encounter,
you deeply dread having to face.
You search for a way up and out of this terrible, dark pit,
Until you hear a sweet, quiet voice saying,
"Be still my child and sit."

"Gloomy it may be with uncertainties all around,
But settle in the assurance of
knowing you're not all alone."

"I am with you every step of the way,
If you continue trusting me, I'll lead you to a brighter day!"

*"The Lord is the one who goes ahead of you; He will be with
you. He will not fail you or forsake you.
Do not fear or be dismayed."*
~Deuteronomy 31:8

"But he said to me, 'My grace is sufficient for you, for my power is made perfect in weakness.' Therefore I will boast all the more gladly about my weaknesses, so that Christ's power may rest on me."
~ 2 Corinthians 12:9 NIV

And He has said to me, "My grace is sufficient for you, for power is perfected in weakness." Most gladly, therefore, I will rather boast about my weaknesses, so that the power of Christ may dwell in me.
~ 2 Corinthians 12:9 NASB

In life, we are frequently visited by hurt, pain, disappointment, heartache and heartbreak. It seems that trials come on every hand and life is filled with swift transitions. When these horrendous and horrifying moments appear, they seem to hit us so hard in our guts that we find ourselves gasping and fighting to catch our breath. The light that was just shining in our lives is immediately overtaken by darkness with an invasion of fear accompanying it. Because of the heaviness of the burden, our straight erected posture collapses as our legs began to buckle and we fall to our knees. It is in this moment, we come to understand that the recognition of our accomplishments from those who applaud, comment, and like what we're doing and saying become obsolete because we are now in our broken state, our lowly state, our vulnerable state, our state where many who gave us praises will pity us or walk away from us. Today, I want you to be encouraged because it is in this very moment, in this very place, in this very state that you come into the experience with God where not only great revelation takes place, but great manifestation takes place. This is when you are in tuned to the right voice and you'll hear God speaking,
"My grace is sufficient for you.
My power is perfected in weakness."

Listen to God speaking to you:

"My grace..." not your works

"My grace..." not your intellect

"My grace..." not your bank account or your financial portfolio

"My grace..." not your husband, honey, boo...

or anyone else you think that makes you look picture perfect

"My grace..." not your job, not your business, not your sorority, not your social club or anything else you think makes you powerful and sustains you...

"My grace is sufficient!"

"Is sufficient"...it's enough, it's adequate, it's all you need. Notice it didn't even have to say more than sufficient because in its sufficiency it's the sum...total! It's full and complete.

What is God's Grace?

It's His favor. It's His kindness.

Grace is a gift of love that invites us into relationship with Him. It's a distributive portion of God that flows through His Son, Jesus the Christ, to us through the Holy Spirit to sanctify us and reside within us, working on us to make us holy and perform supernaturally in and through our lives!

"My grace is sufficient."

"My power is perfected in weakness."

"My power..." my ability, my control,

It's dynamis! It's forceful! It has energy!

If He's represented by the characteristic of His power, having His abilities perfects your inabilities; His control perfects your chaotic whirlwind and rollercoaster ride of life; His forcefulness combats the demons of Hades that you in your own greatest might would be trampled and sifted by: His energy will refuel you when you thought there was no more gas in your tank to go on. His power is made perfect in your weakness!

Grace

Prayer of Purpose:

"Father I stretch my hands to thee, no other help I know. If You withdraw Yourself from me, O whether shall I go."

Dear God, my Father, I've gone to the end of the road where I realize I've exhausted all my options and exerted all other resources in an attempt to try to figure my way out of this predicament. I've come to crossroads and have ended up at dead ends. I've come to intersections and have obviously ended up on paths that didn't lead me to the destination that will help me to rise out of this situation. I've done all I know to do trying to grab onto lifelines floating on the stormy sea of life in which I am drowning. I thank You that before I've decided to throw in the towel, the Holy Spirit sent this to my remembrance that You will supply all my needs according to Your riches in glory. He reminded me that in my weakest state His power is made perfect. I surrender what is left of me. I trust that giving You the broken fragments of my life You have the power to either mend them or throw them away because they are of no further use in my newly restored place.

Thank You that I understand I no longer have to rely on my own intellect to steer my life or to navigate my way through it. Guide me O thy great Jehovah. I am a pilgrim traveling through this barren land. I am weak, but You are mighty. I pray that You will hold me with Your powerful hand. Thank You for making it so that I would not have to die physically to see the manifestation of this revelation; I just have to die to self - self that wants to be in control; self that wants to be self-sustainable and self-reliable. I cry out to You and give myself back to You, Dear God. You're my Creator. I commend, deliver, and give my spirit and will to You. Thank You that all of my this & thats whatever the this & thats are in my life are made perfect. In the name that is perfect and performs perfectly in every way, in Jesus' name, AMEN.

is Sufficient

Your Prayer of Faith

Date: _____

_____

_____

_____

_____

_____

_____

_____

Your Faith Work

Date: _____

_____

_____

_____

_____

_____

_____

_____

Your Faith Praise

Date: _____

_____

_____

_____

_____

_____

_____

_____

"LORD my God, I called to you for help, and you healed me."
~ Psalms 30:2

"I need thee O I need thee, every hour I need thee. O bless me now my Savior, I come to thee."

Prayer of Purpose:

Thank You God *for being ever present. There is no place I can go to escape Your presence. Even when I haven't acknowledged Your presence, You are right here with me. Your Word says, if I make my way to the heavens, there I will find You and even if I make my bed in hell, I'll discover You are there with me also. I know where You are, You are accompanied by Your power to help me and to heal me. So, I pray today as You've met me in this place where I am, if there's any hope, help or healing for me, it will only come through Your powerful hand. I pray that You pull me out of this place I'm entrapped in my mind. Others have desired to help, but they're unable to reach the secret places in my mind. I pray that today, You will guard the gates of my mind. I pray that You free me of every invoking thought that infiltrates my mind causing me to waste away. Guide my feet along the pathway that's free from the deception of beauty because its pathway is filled with thorns that constantly prick me causing hurt, pain, shame, disgust and hopelessness. I thank You because I believe on the other side of the gate is everything You promised me in You. I know there are still tough times I must face. The difference will be me allowing You to be my help for every wound I get as I continue trying to get it right. You are there to soothe the pain and heal me. Thank You in Jesus' name, AMEN.*

Your Prayer of Faith   Date: _____

_____

_____

_____

_____

_____

_____

_____

_____

Your Faith Work   Date: _____

_____

_____

_____

_____

_____

_____

_____

Your Faith Praise   Date: _____

_____

_____

_____

_____

_____

_____

_____

BROKEN

B - BETRAYED

R - RUINED

O - OVERWHELMED

K - KNOCKED DOWN

E - EMPTY

N - NEGLECTED

Healing Scriptures

BETRAYED

"Even my best friend, the one I trusted completely, the one who shared my food, has turned against me." ~ Psalm 41:9

How blessed are those who are persecuted for righteousness' sake, because the kingdom from heaven belongs to them! "How blessed are you whenever people insult you, persecute you, and say all sorts of evil things against you falsely because of me! Rejoice and be extremely glad, because your reward in heaven is great! That's how they persecuted the prophets who came before you."
~ Matthew 5:10-12

For it is not an enemy who insults me— I could have handled that— nor is it someone who hates me and who now arises against me— I could have hidden myself from him— but it is you— a man whom I treated as my equal— my personal confidant, my close friend! We had good fellowship together; and we even walked together in the house of God!
~ Psalm 55:12-14

Bless those who persecute you. Keep on blessing them, and never curse them. Rejoice with those who are rejoicing. Cry with those who are crying. Live in harmony with each other. Do not be arrogant, but associate with humble people. Do not think that you are wiser than you really are. Do not pay anyone back evil for evil, but focus your thoughts on what is right in the sight of all people. If possible, so far as it depends on you, live in peace with all people. Do not take revenge, dear friends, but leave room for God's wrath. For it is written, "Vengeance belongs to me. I will pay them back, declares the Lord."
~ Romans 12:14-19

"My relatives stay far away, and my friends have turned against me. My family is gone, and my close friends have forgotten me."
~ Job 19:13-14

"Even if my father and mother abandon me, the LORD cares for me."
~ Psalm 27:10

"My close friends detest me. Those I loved have turned against me." ~ Job 19:19

"For the more we suffer for Christ, the more God will shower us with his comfort through Christ." ~ 2 Corinthians 1:5

RUINED

"With his mouth the godless man would destroy his neighbor, but by knowledge the righteous are delivered." ~ Proverbs 11:9

"A troublemaker plants seeds of strife; gossip separates the best of friends."
~ Proverbs 16:28

"For the mouth of the wicked and the mouth of the deceitful are opened against me; They have spoken against me with a lying tongue." ~ Psalm 109:2

"They have also surrounded me with words of hatred, And have fought against me without a cause." ~ Psalm 109:3

"Many have become my enemies without cause; those who hate me without reason are numerous." ~Psalm 38:19

"Be still in the presence of the LORD, and wait patiently for him to act. Don't worry about evil people who prosper or fret about their wicked schemes."
~ Psalm 37:7

"But do this in a gentle and respectful way.[a] Keep your conscience clear. Then if people speak against you, they will be ashamed when they see what a good life you live because you belong to Christ." ~ 1 Peter 3:16

"Be kind and helpful to one another, tender-hearted [compassionate, understanding], forgiving one another [readily and freely], just as God in Christ also forgave you." ~ Ephesians 4:32

"Don't repay evil for evil. Don't retaliate with insults when people insult you. Instead, pay them back with a blessing. That is what God has called you to do, and he will grant you his blessing." ~ 1 Peter 3:9

"Bless those who persecute you [who cause you harm or hardship]; bless and do not curse [them]." ~ Romans 12:14

OVERWHELMED

"Be still and know (recognize, understand) that I am God.
I will be exalted among the nations! I will be exalted in the earth."
~Psalm 46:10

"But you belong to God, my dear children. You have already won a victory over those people, because the Spirit who lives in you is greater than the spirit who lives in the world."
~1 John 4:4

" He restores my soul. He leads me in paths of righteousness for his name's sake. Even though I walk through the valley of the shadow of death, I will fear no evil, for you are with me; your rod and your staff, they comfort me."
~ Psalm 23:3-4

"Then Jesus said, "Come to me all of you who are weary and carry heavy burdens, and I will give you rest."~ Matthew 11:28

For I have given rest to the weary and joy to the sorrowing." ~ Jeremiah 31:25

"O God, listen to my cry! Hear my prayer! From the ends of the earth, I cry to you for help when my heart is overwhelmed. Lead me to the towering rock of safety, for you are my safe refuge, a fortress where my enemies cannot reach me. Let me live forever in your sanctuary, safe beneath the shelter of your wings! ~ Psalm 61:1-4

"I am leaving you with a gift—peace of mind and heart. And the peace I give is a gift the world cannot give. So don't be troubled or afraid. "~ John 14:27

"You will keep in perfect peace all who trust in you, all whose thoughts are fixed on you!"
~ Isaiah 26:3

"Cast your burden on the Lord [release it] and He will sustain and uphold you;
He will never allow the righteous to be shaken (slip, fall, fail)." ~ Psalm 55:22

"Do not be anxious or worried about anything, but in everything [every circumstance and situation] by prayer and petition with thanksgiving, continue to make your [specific] requests known to God. And the peace of God [that peace which reassures the heart, that peace] which transcends all understanding, [that peace which] stands guard over your hearts and your minds in Christ Jesus [is yours]." ~ Philippians 4:6-7

"Call on Me in the day of trouble;
I will rescue you, and you shall honor and glorify Me." ~ Psalm 50:15

"Trust in and rely confidently on the Lord with all your heart And do not rely on your own insight or understanding. In all your ways know and acknowledge and recognize Him,
And He will make your paths straight and smooth [removing obstacles that block your way]." ~ Proverbs 3:5-6

"In conclusion, be strong in the Lord [draw your strength from Him and be empowered through your union with Him] and in the power of His [boundless] might." ~Ephesians 6:10

"For I can do everything through Christ, who gives me strength."
~ Philippians 4:13

"But Jesus looked at them and said, "With people [as far as it depends on them] it is impossible, but with God all things are possible." ~Matthew 19:26

KNOCKED DOWN

"Dear friends, don't be surprised at the fiery trials you are going through, as if something strange were happening to you. 13 Instead, be very glad—for these trials make you partners with Christ in his suffering, so that you will have the wonderful joy of seeing his glory when it is revealed to all the world."
~ 1 Peter 4:12-13

"So be truly glad.[a] There is wonderful joy ahead, even though you must endure many trials for a little while. 7 These trials will show that your faith is genuine. It is being tested as fire tests and purifies gold—though your faith is far more precious than mere gold. So when your faith remains strong through many trials, it will bring you much praise and glory and honor on the day when Jesus Christ is revealed to the whole world." ~ 1 Peter 1:6-7

"We are pressed on every side by troubles, but we are not crushed. We are perplexed, but not driven to despair. We are hunted down, but never abandoned by God. We get knocked down, but we are not destroyed. Through suffering, our bodies continue to share in the death of Jesus so that the life of Jesus may also be seen in our bodies. Yes, we live under constant danger of death because we serve Jesus, so that the life of Jesus will be evident in our dying bodies."
~ 2 Corinthians 4:8-11

"Then call on me when you are in trouble, and I will rescue you, and you will give me glory." ~ Psalm 50:15

"When I am in distress, I call to you, because you answer me." ~ Psalm 86:7

"Be strong and let your hearts take courage,
All you who wait for and confidently expect the Lord." ~ Psalm 31:24

"But my God shall supply all your need according to his riches in glory by Christ Jesus." ~ Philippians 4:19

"And I am certain that God, who began the good work within you, will continue his work until it is finally finished on the day when Christ Jesus returns."
~ Philippians 1:6

"He gives strength to the weary,
And to him who has no might He increases power." ~ Isaiah 40:29

"The Lord will fight for you while you [only need to] keep silent and remain calm."
~ Exodus 14:14

He rescued us from so great a threat of death, and will continue to rescue us. On Him we have set our hope. And He will again rescue us [from danger and draw us near], ~ 2 Corinthians 1:10

"Yet I am confident I will see the Lord's goodness while I am here in the land of the living. Wait patiently for the Lord. Be brave and courageous. Yes, wait patiently for the Lord." ~ Psalm 27:13-14

"I waited patiently for the LORD to help me, and he turned to me and heard my cry. He lifted me out of the pit of despair, out of the mud and the mire. He set my feet on solid ground and steadied me as I walked along." ~ Psalm 40:1-2

"I have been young and now I am old,
Yet I have not seen the righteous (those in right standing with God) abandoned
Or his descendants pleading for bread." ~ Psalm 37:25

"I have told you these things, so that in Me you may have [perfect] peace. In the world you have tribulation and distress and suffering, but be courageous [be confident, be undaunted, be filled with joy]; I have overcome the world." [My conquest is accomplished, My victory abiding.]" ~ John 16:33

"For I am the LORD your God who takes hold of your right hand and says to you, Do not fear; I will help you."~ Isaiah 41:13

"The LORD is my light and my salvation— whom will I fear? The LORD is the strength of my life; of whom will I be afraid?" ~ Psalm 27:1

"The Lord is my rock, my fortress, and the One who rescues me; My God, my rock and strength in whom I trust and take refuge;
My shield, and the horn of my salvation, my high tower—my stronghold."
~ Psalm 18:2

"The temptations in your life are no different from what others experience. And God is faithful. He will not allow the temptation to be more than you can stand. When you are tempted, he will show you a way out so that you can endure."
~ 1 Corinthians 10:13

EMPTY

"The LORD is the one who is going ahead of you. He will be with you. He won't abandon you or leave you. So don't be afraid or terrified." ~ Deuteronomy 31:8

"He said, "My presence will go with you, and I'll give you rest." ~ Exodus 33:14

"Be strong and courageous. Don't fear or tremble before them, because the LORD your God will be the one who keeps on walking with you—he won't leave you or abandon you."
~ Deuteronomy 31:6

"The righteous cry out, and the Lord hears, and delivers them from all their troubles. The Lord is near the brokenhearted; He saves those crushed in spirit." ~ Psalm 34:17-18

"Don't be afraid, because I'm with you; don't be anxious, because I am your God. I keep on strengthening you; I'm truly helping you. I'm surely upholding you with my victorious right hand." ~ Isaiah 41:10

"Therefore we do not lose heart, but though our outer man is decaying, yet our inner man is being renewed day by day."
~ 2 Corinthians 4:16

"For our present troubles are small and won't last very long. Yet they produce for us a glory that vastly outweighs them and will last forever! 18 So we don't look at the troubles we can see now; rather, we fix our gaze on things that cannot be seen. For the things we see now will soon be gone, but the things we cannot see will last forever."
~2 Corinthians 4:17-18

"For I consider [from the standpoint of faith] that the sufferings of the present life are not worthy to be compared with the glory that is about to be revealed to us and in us!" ~ Romans 8:18

"In my distress I called to the LORD, and He answered and set me free."
~ Psalm 118:5

NEGLECTED

"Because you are precious in My sight,
You are honored and I love you, I will give other men in return for
you and other peoples in exchange for your life." ~ Isaiah 43:4

"For I know the plans and thoughts that I have for you,' says the Lord,
'plans for peace and well-being and not for disaster, to give you a
future and a hope." ~ Jeremiah 29:11

The LORD will work out his plans for my life—for your faithful love, O
LORD, endures forever. Don't abandon me, for you made me.
~ Psalm 138:8

"And we know [with great confidence] that God [who is deeply
concerned about us] causes all things to work together [as a plan] for
good for those who love God, to those who are called according to
His plan and purpose."
~ Romans 8:28-29

"Now you are no longer a slave but God's own child. And since you
are his child, God has made you his heir." ~ Galatians 4:7

"You were bought with a price [you were actually purchased with the
precious blood of Jesus and made His own]. So then, honor and
glorify God with your body." ~1 Corinthians 6:20

"But forget all that—it is nothing compared to what I am going to do.
For I am about to do something new. See, I have already begun! Do
you not see it? I will make a pathway through the wilderness. I will
create rivers in the dry wasteland." ~ Isaiah 43:18-19

"How Long"

How long must I hurt so deeply Dear Lord
When you have the power to say, "Be gone"?
How long must I travel this road dark and eerie all
alone?
How long must I cry myself to sleep
making myself think how foolish I am when I
repeatedly say, "Girl come on,
you don't have to weep"?
How long will this last,
will you please Lord let it pass?
How long Lord?
How long?

*"Weeping may endure for a night but joy comes
in the morning."*
~Psalm 30:5

"LORD, be gracious to us; we long for you. Be our strength every morning, our salvation in time of distress." ~ Isaiah 33:2

When we humbly present ourselves to the all righteous, loving, merciful God, we will find His immeasurable graciousness. With the awakening of each new day, we experience the new mercies of God. Every day because of His faithfulness, we can depend on our daily bread being provided to us. Because each day will have trials and tribulations, we must have renewed strength for these battles. So every morning, we should begin requesting God to be gracious to us. As we've spent 9 eventful moments together "Being Healed", we are living witnesses to the power of God's almighty hand that has kept us. We are now Exhibits of His salvation. We are saved, set free and healed!

Prayer of Purpose:

Dear God full of love, grace and mercy, I thank You for being my Jehovah Rapha, You have healed me. I know if You had left me to myself when I was acting out and turning away from You, thinking I had the ingenuity to do things and take care of matters myself, I would be finished. If I wasn't overtaken by my situations, I would have self destructed. I pray with the dawning of each new day; I will lift my eyes unto the hills from whence comes my help knowing that all of my help comes from You. I pray each day as I commit myself to You and Your assignment in the day, You will give me strength to carry it out. I need You to arise with me O God. I know my enemies can't stand Your powerful presence. May I be steadfast in Your ways and use all the power you've given me to walk victoriously overcoming everything in this world, even the sting of death and the grave. Thank you for being my strong tower, in Jesus' name, AMEN.

Your Prayer of Faith   Date: _____

_____

_____

_____

_____

_____

_____

_____

Your Faith Work   Date: _____

_____

_____

_____

_____

_____

_____

_____

Your Faith Praise   Date: _____

_____

_____

_____

_____

_____

_____

_____

My Healing Has Been Delivered

"My flesh and my heart may fail, but God is the strength of my heart and my portion forever."

~ Psalms 73:26

It's true, frail is humanity, short is life and these days are full of trouble yet, God will not withhold any good thing from you.

My Healing Declaration

I remember at the age of 12, I was singing one of my favorite songs by my songbird, Sarah Jordan Powell, "He Touched Me." This particular time, I began singing the verse with great conviction - *"Shackled by a heavy burden, beneath a load of guilt and shame..."* and then with the strongest desire, I set out to proclaim with all my might - *"then the hand of Jesus touched me and now I am no longer the same."* I must be honest, as a child I can't recall anything in my life that I could point to causing the shackling of a heavy burden or such overpowering guilt and shame. Today, I better understand because in my becoming, is the essence of my being. In other words, I was living in my being **(present/future)** while I was becoming. *My Healing Declaration* is that yes, I have had many tears and sorrows and I have had questions about my tomorrows. I have seen some really grand days, but I've also had days where I was living in a nightmare while wide awake. But this became my Faith Declaration - that although there are *many things about tomorrow, I don't seem to understand, I know who holds my tomorrow and I know He holds my hand. The one holding my hand is the One* in control of everything; there's nothing He and I couldn't handle together. So, I professed, *"Because He lives, I can face tomorrow, Because He lives, all fear is gone; Because I know He holds my future, My life is worth the living, Just because He lives!"*

I know that my inflictions, whether brought on by self or others and the state I've found myself, did not define me; it didn't cause me to forfeit my destiny or altar my final destination. I believed the wonderful plans God had for me, when I was just a thought in His mind, would really happen. So, instead of pouting and pitying myself, I praised God! Instead of crumbling under the pressures of life. I chose to champion life - mustering up every ounce of strength and courage to clear every hurdle. It didn't matter if I got tripped up or fell and had to get back up in excruciating pain with opened wounds, blood flowing, embarrassment and pain, I was determined to stay the course and finish the race. I refused to let my brokenness disqualify me from the race. I rehearsed my favorite and most promising scripture saying, "Therefore, my beloved brethren, be ye steadfast, unmovable, always abounding in the work of the Lord, forasmuch as ye know that your labor is not in vain in the Lord." ~ 1 Corinthians 15:58 I believed God!

So, while in the labor room, my birthing coach, the Holy Spirit, urged me to keep praying, to keep pushing, to keep praising and to keep proclaiming...now birthed is my healing! "Thank God For It All" (as Marvin Sapp expresses my deepest sentiment)

Totally Praising,
Tanya

Your Healing Declaration

Date: _____

_____

_____

_____

_____

_____

_____

_____

_____

_____

_____

_____

_____

_____

_____

My love, I present this Rose to you...

Why a white rose you might wonder...? The white rose my friend while it's beautiful to behold, is more than a showcase of sheer beauty. Its pure white color conveys an expression of peace and love. It's used to pay homage to new starts and expresses hope for the future.

So, how befitting is this? Your healing welcomes you into a newness of life. What was killing you inside causing a death trap has been forced to release you. You are presented as a new creature bidding a farewell to the old things that were sucking life from you and welcoming the breath of your promising present and future that births life greater than you've known before. Your latter shall be greater than your past. Remember God's plans are always to prosper you and not for your demise. Walk gracefully in your new life. You are no longer broken, you are whole. **Jehovah Rapha has healed you!**

Love & Peace
Tonya

Made in the USA
Coppell, TX
06 February 2021